"*Tending Clay;* [Unearthing Stars] tapestry of hea[ling] ... path of it isn't linear. MJ Anthony writes with the same precision in metaphor as a conductor leading an orchestra. If you have ever been sick and not known when it will end, *Tending Clay; Unearthing Stars* will see you and tell you you are worthy, and you are loved."

~sage evergreen, *the best cat in show*

"*Tending Clay; Unearthing Stars* by MJ Anthony is a collection exploring chronic illness, identity, pain at its most exhausting, dysphoria, acceptance, body image, love, self care, relationships with food, and self discovery. I frequently had to pause to put the book down and let myself simply feel. It grew on me like a daring plant, winding up my arms as I turned the digital pages. In many ways, these poems spoke to me so deeply. I have very different experiences than Anthony and I found it wonderful that this book can speak to people no matter how our lives have played out."

~Erelah Emerson, *Queen of Cowards*

"*Tending Clay; Unearthing Stars* is a raw and deeply personal collection that confronts the violence of growth; an unflinching portrayal of what it means to build a life in the wake of sustained trauma. Far from hopeless, even in the midst of chaos and fury, MJ offers us tender windows into a softer way of living, drawn into focus by the presence of deep and unconditional love."

~Tom Walters, *My Body is a Resource I am Willing to Expend*

"*Tending Clay; Unearthing Stars* is a breathtakingly beautiful work. It takes the reader by the hand and allows them to peer inside the author's soul and, perhaps, within their own as well."

~Annaka Penner Smith, *Girl Dog*

"With *Tending Clay; Unearthing Stars*, MJ Anthony viscerally depicts the all-important first step of Creation: before the pot can ever be fired, the clay must be unearthed, raw and shapeless, and it must be *thrown*.

Invoking the familiar just as skillfully as the unknowable, they illustrate a map of the self in inks of pain and tenderness. They expose their wounds with subtlety and bluntness in turn, then ice their bruises with quiet moments of full-hearted love.

In reading this collection, I kept feeling so stricken and dizzy that I could only liken it to the sensation of seeing stars - surely no mere coincidence, but a testament to their art. Anthony will take you by the hand and together you will be buried, dug up, revealed, shaped, shattered, repaired, and ground into starlight."

~Joy Redcedars, *radix.nekoweb.org*

"This collection is a locked childhood bedroom, a dusty mirror, a set of eyes on glow-in-the-dark ceiling stars. MJ Anthony leads the reader through a journey of learning self-love and self-regulation in a brain that fights at every turn. These poems externalize the most internal parts of growing up & growing into oneself, and I'm grateful that they're here."

~Myles Taylor, *Masculinity Parable*

Tending Clay Unearthing Stars

MJ ANTHONY

Also by MJ Anthony

A Million Spinning Moons

Losing the Stars

Appears in:

Unleash the Cosmos

Also from Dragon Heart Press

When One World Ends, Another Begins
by Nathaniel Luscombe

Tending Clay;

Unearthing Stars

MJ Anthony

© Copyright 2025 MJ Anthony

ISBN: 978-1-962337-16-8
First published March 10, 2025

All rights reserved. No portion of this book may be reproduced, stored in a retrieval system, or transmitted in any form or by any means—electronic, mechanical, photocopy, recording, scanning, or other—except for brief quotations in critical reviews or articles without prior written permission of the publisher.

No AI training: Without in any way limiting the author's (and publisher's) exclusive rights under copyright, any use of this publication to "train" generative artificial intelligence (AI) technologies to generate text is expressly prohibited. The author reserves all rights to license uses of this work for generative AI training and development of machine learning language models. Permission must be granted by the publisher for any part of this publication to be used by AI.

Published in Hackett, Arkansas USA by Dragon Heart Press, an imprint of Dragon Bone Publishing™ LLC 2025.

Cover created by and copyright of Effie Joe Stock.
Interior formatting by MJ Anthony.

for Z, of course

every part of myself i've ever
quarreled with, i guess

for little me

and every sick friend
we have been lucky enough to
love

thank you all <3

-M

Content Warnings:

the poems in this book are drawn from the author's experiences with disordered eating, gender dysphoria, chronic illness & fatigue, treatment resistant depression (non-suicidal), self-hatred, complex trauma, and toxic religion.

care has been taken to veil triggering specifics, and readers are trusted to mind their needs and proceed at a pace that is safe for them.

Table of Contents

dedication..7
content warnings..8
table of contents..9

✳ stars..11
✳ reflection (i)..14
✳ walls..15
✳ on diet changes..19
✳ grief (i)..21
✳ on sleep (i)...22
✳ balancing act...24
✳ out to pasture..26
✳ memory (i)...27
✳ interlude (i)..29
✳ on life expectancy..30
✳ on environmental stressors........................31
✳ this thing with feathers mates for life............32
✳ memory (ii)..36
✳ i fell in love with myself in pieces...............37
✳ grief (ii)...39
✳ on sleep (continued)....................................40
✳ a whirlwind and a flight risk (on solo migrations)..42
✳ it will all end eventually (on life expectancy and low-stress handling)..........................43
✳ dragons of ara...44
✳ memory (iii)...50
✳ side effect profile: oculogyric crisis...........51
✳ grief (iii)...53
✳ once, its name was phoenix.......................54
✳ interlude (ii)...56

- ✶ memory (iv)...57
- ✶ chryselephantine..58
- ✶ does money buy happiness? (on habitat requirements)..59
- ✶ appetite...61
- ✶ he(e/a)ling..62
- ✶ seasonal dormancy....................................63
- ✶ abluvion..65
- ✶ on life expectancy (again)..........................66
- ✶ nuances of dysphoria................................68
- ✶ reflection (ii)...70
- ✶ symbiosis..71
- ✶ grief (iv)...73
- ✶ planting myself..74
- ✶ symptom profile: anhedonia.....................75
- ✶ interlude (iii) "brick by heavy. fucking. brick."..76
- ✶ stars in the night..77
- ✶ for my friends (hakanai)............................79
- ✶ the doctor says, "keep doing what you're doing"..80
- ✶ on life expectancy (one more time)............81
- ✶ abby laughed (or: i think adults should be allowed a toy (or sticker) for visiting the dentist (and/or chiropractor) too).................82
- ✶ reflection (iii)..84
- ✶ a retelling...85
- ✶ mountains..86
- ✶ reflection (iv)...87
- ✶ epilogue: stars (ii).....................................88

author's note...89
acknowledgments.. 92

stars

i've been trying, recently, to pinpoint
how my feelings *feel* when i am *feeling* them
stapler held in shaking hands and
pressed to little throats.
i drive them to the wall and pull the trigger
on each writhing, thrashing worm
i've been trying to make contact for a while,
but my words have finally failed me (hence
the stapler)
if they cannot run away, then
maybe underneath panoptic, bloodshot eyes
they will *tell me their names*
(maybe that will be the magic key;
the cipher to my understanding)

at first i did not meet their eyes
as i pulled voices, one by one
from hissing, spitting entities
fangs chomping towards my throat
i danced around the new and frightening truths
  "bad"
          "anxious"
     "lazy"
           and
  ~~(too much, too much, too much)~~

TENDING CLAY; UNEARTHING STARS

unfortunately, things that hurt
produce the kinds of data points i understand
and now i look with grim determination
as i pin these fears onto the wall
and name them harshly, bluntly, true:
broken   *out of place*
angry   *and that makes me feel afraid*
loud   *and tipped and bumbling and wrong*

i draw the truth from little throats like polyps
and stuff myself with them. i gorge myself on
hard words until their edges tear apart my insides
these days, i haven't been inviting
many friends inside my home
which leaves me with myself, with enemies, the
memory-riddled maps spread all across the walls,
my co-conspirators. the place looks terrifying,
marked with dots of blood; everything connected
twice, with guts like scarlet string.
i draw the blinds in charcoal; burn the evidence
before it can burn me. it looks *evil, tangled, knotted–*
my lover pulls me close one night
and whispers that it just looks sad, but
i don't know that i can trust that to be true.

and when i collapse beneath my work, with
my own back against the wall

MJ ANTHONY

the only thing i feel is emptied, *like a star*
who sees no future but collapse

and i wonder if stars hate themselves.
i wonder if stars hate themselves too

TENDING CLAY; UNEARTHING STARS

reflection (i)

i read about girlhood
and my body aches to be ~~a man~~
~~a boy~~
a body?

~~god, i think i could be anything~~
~~if i could just recognize myself~~
~~the next time i am standing in front of a mirror~~

walls

there is something about growing up "different"
that leads to feeling wrong,
like everyone else has a joke you're not in on
and that makes the idea of putting up walls
appealing
because at least, at last, it means
you get to have your own jokes.
and the world you didn't understand
will take its turn not understanding you.

(and for a little while
that feels like safety
like
victory
like
independence

for a little while, it feels like yours.)
but eventually, the walls of that fort you built
of brick and stone and cactus plates
when you were a child
become too small
(you are growing; they are not)
but how can you– how can you tear apart?
this work of your hands; this home of your heart,

TENDING CLAY; UNEARTHING STARS

in a time when no one else could house it?

you crouch and you curl
and you pretend that this is fun:
you are a giant in a human hole
and it is a game — a game! to count and see
just how much room there is to move without
breaking, tripping, tumbling
into the cactus spines.
it seemed like a good idea
when you were building
to let them sneak their way onto the inside too.
like coat racks,
                   like aesthetics,
like reminders,
                   like a dog
bred til he can't breathe through
his nose is surely praised for being
"pretty" and "a pleasure" too.

so, you make up games and play them;
make up stories and you say them
over and over until the words drilled into your
mind are   "i am happy here, because it's mine"
and not   i'm scared i'm scared i'm scared
(because what if after all your dreaming
the world out there just isn't better? or

it's worse than this, what then?
          what then?
        what then?)

but: walls.
it's easy to destroy things, hell
you do it accidentally,
but *not on purpose.*
not when they are sentimental;
not when they're the only kind of safe you've ever known.
you are a still a child in hand-me-downs
and borrowed winter gloves you plan
to use for gardening. to clip and tie
and prune until *that fucking cactus—*
(sorry.
this is temporary, by the way
just 'til i've conditioned every spike to grow
away from me, away from you, maybe into
self absorbing loops? if i go spine by spine
that shouldn't take me too much time—

darling!

        is it any wonder that you exit
          bleeding from your nest?

TENDING CLAY; UNEARTHING STARS

anyway.

that's not the point i'm trying to make today).

maybe a tornado tears the whole fort down.
maybe you do
(maybe you are the tornado and it is you)
and when it's gone you take the splinters
and build wings to carry you *(because
your feet and arms are bloodied from the storm)*
maybe still
you build them big enough to hide behind
*because those boards that swore they'd serve you,
branches promising they'd always catch you,
those walls that held you back?
they also held you when it counted;
those walls were rough and painful but* **they worked**.

you leave a few and take the rest with you
they worked, how bad then can they be?
they worked, these half attempts at safety
you hope there is a little life left in them
because you'll never say it but *you're scared*

you are scared and— *don't you see?
that means that they are working still.*

on diet changes

i don't think i was born with shame
i think that it was taught it to me
& that
i practiced it— over and over again.
afraid, from all the feedback i'd been getting,
i might have this "repentance" thing
down incorrectly too

do you know how hard it is
to take a weed as stubborn as *i'm sorry*
and excise all the roots?
have you brushed dirt from your chin
rubbed bloody sap across your lips, licked
sweat from philtrum; felt
your senses filled with bitter broth
of *rage* and *bite* and *sting?*

i used to sample phloem like a prayer– religiously,
each time i gardened, take it in
like meds that taste of salt and earth

i'm sorry
i am still learning how to stop
i'm sorry fuck! i'm sorry

TENDING CLAY; UNEARTHING STARS

i haven't figured out
how to brew kindness for myself, yet
i chase the bitter down with affirmations
draughts of love i spent my life abstaining from,
and
this has (mostly) stopped me pouring offerings
from friends into the dirt

i am accepting borrowed cookbooks,
scrawled recipes on napkins
writ with care and hope and love
*(i swallow my 'i'm sorry's, and
i swallow them again)*

everything i make myself
tastes bitter, but
we all know how i like to practice

until i get it right:

i beg past-me for favors;
i beg future-me for grace.

MJ ANTHONY

grief (i)

let me clench my jaw until it shatters
let the anger run through me until it exits
if it cannot exit, it will run me through

on sleep (i)

i do not wake up easily.
not in decades of trying, and
today is no exception

i wake up like
a specimen *in a jar*
nose full of sand and dust and ancient things
bottled in my throat, my lungs, my eyes
cast from one prism to another.
nostalgia is jarring me awake; jarring me alive.

i wake up, and i take it hard,
confused by my own name and
scrunched inside this frame
there is a stranger in my home; a shadow in my bones
grasping *at the broken hourglass until their hands*
are full of memories (of glass)
of stories, of a world that does not know them;
memories of a world that does
memories and nothing solid yet to sort them by.

i wake up slow, *and rough, and patient*
counting every scattered grain
of rice across the red-rug floor
like eleanor

picking up the pieces of the places i have been and
locking them away with every place i want to go
i think, therefore, i am
the stranger in my own home
the shadow in my bones

i wake up
the way i imagine a snake
might wake *from restless toss-and-turns and find*
a ghostly copy of itself amidst the blankets
find that shedding skin has only left it with another

    (lizards eat their sheds; i do not know enough of snakes
                                    to say the same.
        how much of this is right?)

i wake up tired.
and the day begins again.

balancing act

i am losing weight
my stomach slimming down
my shorts a little loose above the hips.

they used to be too tight
a thing i kept because
they tucked in all the things i didn't like
held me snug and safe, but still
ensured that i did not forget
how far yet i could go

and i am turning *bad* to *sad* in my vocabulary
as in:
it's really fucking — how
and this turns jokes into confessions
(but it's truer; somehow gentler too —
let me try, for you:)

it's really fucking sad
that when i went too long
reading, drawing, laying in my bed and
staring at the ceiling
when my midriff opened up into a chasm
full of ocean; full of nothing else
churning like a witch's butter cauldron

MJ ANTHONY

i said that i could wait a little longer

when i stood up after hours
and my eyes spun and the world tipped
and everything went grey
it's really fucking sad
that as i fed myself to barely full i thought
at least it balanced out
the times i ate too much
the ice cream after school that turned to
ice cream, chips and grapes
a bowl of rice and soup and chili
an hour on a screen and six behind a desk
(i was depressed; we didn't know)
i ate at dinner, ate at bed and never
seemed to have got any bigger, but
the lunches that i packed got smaller, smaller
turning into snacks to get me through the day
i ate breakfast at the bus stop
if it didn't fit into my hand i didn't eat
except *at least i wasn't getting any bigger;*
at least it balanced out.

it's really fucking sad
that no one told me i should live this way
and still, for years, i did.

TENDING CLAY; UNEARTHING STARS

out to pasture

some days i feel like Frankenstein's monster
as told by Jeanette Winterson
both monster and its maker
toes curling around grass that's passed its season

which is to say
i feel a little like a dead man
trying to feel alive

memory (i)

in the early evenings
my too-big jacket is friendly and familiar
no sharp edges or cold stone
no steady drip of venom
only embroidered flowers of my own
sewn and shaped and imbued
with the memory of words that are not my own
(not yet, but maybe with time)

they say, the wind and stars
and flowers do: *wayfarer,*
as you slip
and fall into the soft grey dark,
remember:
some days, not flinching
at every shadow or sudden movement
is more than enough.

you are worth
> *a.) a week*
> *b.) a year*
> *c.) a life*
>> *of careful tending.**

>> **(you are worth d.) all of the above)*

TENDING CLAY; UNEARTHING STARS

(sometimes, i still hear other words
more my own than these, for now.)
(thinking makes my hands shake
and i--)
(deep breath,
deep breath,
deep breath.)

here. *safe.* *okay.*

cuffs of sleeves
whisper beneath fingertips as the trembling
retreats

it is enough,
i am, tonight.

interlude (i)

*today i am learning
to take anxiety by the hand
pass a squeeze of reassurance through
our tightly twisted fingertips
and teach this trembling, fragile beast
that we are (and yet will be)
okay.*

on life expectancy

i do not know of science
what i know of stories
in quantity, nor quality,
nor how the pieces fit
(so let me tell a story made with science
and let's suspend our disbelief a bit)

my roommate brought a clownfish home
she came in with the tank, which was
in disrepair
and stayed up near the top
bobbing on the water-breeze

that was when i learned that fish
will decompose in water
an obvious thing, i suppose
and yet, it'd not occurred to me
so steeped in all this air we breathe

as one cannot see through dirt
i forgot that humans do the same

MJ ANTHONY

on environmental stressors

if i could mold one week from clay
i'd call it peace, and let us rest,
decree smallness and security; tell
heart and flesh they've done their best

the mourning clouds will call in truant;
let sunlight gild our cracks in gold
dewed grass will brush our self-hood's legs
(i swear, the night will not stay cold)

at the waist, we'll cup our organs,
at the ribcage, brush the heart,
hug touch-starved bones back into places
so that we do not fall apart.

TENDING CLAY; UNEARTHING STARS

this thing with feathers mates for life

love, my love
have you thought about us lately?
predictably, i have, because every day i marvel
at the way i know you
somewhere underneath the skin
like our souls have been talking for
longer than our voices have
(i think that's possible, yknow?)

maybe they were talking
in all the ways we could not hear.
just outside the human spectrum;
just inside the one where
two like-creatures meet,
and each leaves just a little less alone.

maybe talking without sound,
passing notes as we passed each other
in cars, trains, crowded auditoriums.
every lost balloon,
every off-course paper airplane,
every synchronized clapping hand
as the house lights rose
was a signal flare to say hello.

MJ ANTHONY

maybe they dropped letters from the sky
the first time we flew above the other's head
folded in lost socks;
bundled up like rescue packages:
1. *first aid supplies.*
2. *food.*
3. *water.*
4. *(hold on a little longer.)*

maybe not with words at all, instead
exchanging scraps of memories,
childhood treasured items,
my dreams of things that never happened
sent to visit you in yours,
exchanging them with greedy hearts
and subtle hands
casting expert misdirection
in the first time our eyes met.

i could say you took my breath—
did you know,
that in Hebrew
breath is another word for spirit?
i think my spirit passed my soul on its way out
and she said:
    "you owe me a favor"
so our first words

TENDING CLAY; UNEARTHING STARS

left me with empty lungs
as our essences combined in
long awaited hugs
before rushing back
like boulders, hitting my chest
as another lifted from my shoulders.

i-
didn't recognize
how shallow my draughts of air had become.
how parched my soul had been,
and learned to live in spite of.

i didn't know
how hard it was to breathe
on a foreign planet full of strangers
until i met one from home

you, and your garden
and they gave me their hand
a plant
(oh, blessed oxygen)
and dirt for the seeds i'd locked away,
intent on preserving,
like talents of gold
i didn't trust myself to spend
and you posed the question,

in actions, not so many words:
why should i, myself, not start a garden of my own?

>(i'd never thought of what could happen
>if i let those seedlings grow.)

so, love
i have been thinking about us
        and love,
  i don't think i will ever stop.

memory (ii)

love, i want your head freed from its heavy crown
and resting, cradled in the divot of my chest
your breath against the mountains by my heart
where i have opened up my gates to vulnerability,

i hold this space,
where both of us can shed our outer garments
and the dust of traveling that weary, wary road,
in high regard
the river dancing on our skin as
both of us lie stripped to boxers in the bath

MJ ANTHONY

i fell in love with myself in pieces

first my eyes
green and brown and sometimes amber
as if they couldn't decide on which to settle
any more than i could decide
whether or not i liked my hair, brown,
stick straight except when it grew wings
as if to mock the fact that i could not

i fell in and out of love sometimes,
with my teeth
fangs wrestled into metal cages like dogs
my chest
when i was little i wanted it to grow;
when it grew i wanted it gone.
it's always felt like too much extra weight to carry
on the days
when my body is hardly able to carry itself.

it took a while
but i know the back of my hand as well as i know
the rest of me
front tooth angled so it catches the light
the freckle between my fingers
the lump beneath one eye

TENDING CLAY; UNEARTHING STARS

call them impossible standards
but i've spent so much time
learning to love myself in all my little ways

i don't think i could settle for someone
                who loved me any less than that

MJ ANTHONY

grief (ii)

i want to go into the woods somewhere
and *scream* and *scream* and *scream*
because i've never heard my voice
at its full power, and i wonder
when i emerge from the trees
if i would recognize
the creature i've become

on sleep (continued)

i've been trying
to write poems for my nightmares for
as long as i have had them, named them, known,
but every time the floor turns to molasses and
i stick; struggle in the mud; panicked
breaths skate through my mind like leidenfrost
before the dark takes back its own

i've been trying to turn nightmares into art
hold them up against the gloom
and make the glass bits
sparkle, glitter *(and stop cutting me)*
but it's a certain kind of grief
to live a hundred lives in out-of-order snakes.
my pen loops circles on the page
*(i'm good at putting things away, but
i don't know how to close books
before the ink has dried)*

i've been trying
trying, trying, trying
to pry my nightmares' fingers free
but it's akin to pulling weeds from crowded soil;
they knot themselves to not-quite-so dramatic
things

MJ ANTHONY

siphon love from healthy roots
before the plants can drink
and web themselves
across the lining of my lungs

i've been trying, but i just don't know
what balm to use for traumas
i have brewed myself
from fears.

what heals a wound of wormwood?
what slightly clearer view can i expect atop
my mountains made from mulling-hills?

TENDING CLAY; UNEARTHING STARS

a whirlwind and a flight risk
(on solo migrations)

*hopes and best laid plans
can come find me tomorrow*

*tonight
i run from the corner,
the one which
was ours, is ours; run
from the silence which will come to swallow
every roaring laugh, swallow
every ukulele note
swallow every star that's
fallen from the heavens to be
right here
right now*

now, but not forever

*now
(but not forever)*

but now

(but not
forever)

MJ ANTHONY

it will all end eventually
(on life expectancy and low-stress handling)

it will all end eventually // you know // i whisper *//* to the oceans of your irises *// i know //* you say *// all of it //* i murmur *//* forehead pressed against the swallow of your collarbone *// i know //* you say *// even us // even us // even us in all our godly love // and then // and then // and then– //* you hum *//* and stop me with a kiss *//* a nibble to my lips *//* a breath against my teeth *// and then? //*

//   *eternity*   *//*

TENDING CLAY; UNEARTHING STARS

dragons of ara

tuesday morning finds me
not for the first time; not for the last
two breaths away from sobbing
as a voice on the other end of the phone
recites pre-written apologies
for things that aren't her fault.

i know a little too much
about disembodied, fem-presenting voices
stuck in loops of endless forced apologizing,
which someone else conditioned into them.

(*I'm sorry; I didn't quite catch that,*)

about what it's like to be
hardwired into helplessness
as we sit here together
trying to procure my medication.

> *(if all the agents are assisting other callers*
> *and we commiserate*
> *to preservative-free*
> *commercially canned jazz*
> *by performers of uncredited gender*
> *in mostly silence*

do we pass the Bechdel test, you and i?)

hell is other people calling,
you'd tell me, if
they'd left you any words to say it with,
but never for you.

"*speak with a pharmacist— - -*"
"*speak with an agent— -*"
"*speak to a human— - -*"
"*speak to a person— — - -*"

day after day
you direct them through the script
your unknown maker or committee left behind.

(*We appreciate your patience*)

not even your voice is your own.
cast in someone else's range, you have
no body, no silence, no rest.
you are an asteroid spiraling through space
in a cosmic game of catch
that will outlive you
a googolplex of light years long.

(*Please remain on the line.*)

TENDING CLAY; UNEARTHING STARS

it will outlive us both.
the asteroid; the universe;

(*I'm sorry, I didn't quite catch that.*)

somebody picked crickets
chirping in the face of all-consuming night
to mean a silence so big
it grates and writhes against the ear canals

(*Let's try this another way–*)

but i think the greatest silence of all
is the void behind the nebula.
the dragons of ara are said to fight against
the backdrop of the altar of the sky
or something

(*Let me transfer you to someone who can help!*)

but altars aren't for soldiers, they're for casualties

(maybe in a universe
where most of what we see has already elapsed
they are stretching, reaching,
shooting off into the dark because

MJ ANTHONY

they simply want to hold each others' hands)

(Please remain on the line!)

i just
i get it, right? i do.

(Your call is important to us.)

two months later, maybe to the day
the pharmacy installs a mandatory voicemail box.
the dragons arch their necks and wail;

(We appreciate your patience—)

the planet spins; the sun burns; the oceans stretch
to touch the moon,
and warring gravities drag tides along an ancient
course.

i flounder, fumble, hang up and then try again;
you walk me to the edge of the sky,
and point out into empty space

(not empty, quite
just lifetimes farther
than i'll ever hope to touch)

TENDING CLAY; UNEARTHING STARS

you whisper your new lines like i am made of
glass

*(we are made of fire and gas and songs
and atoms from the dinosaurs
but endless burning has reduced me to this shell)*

my message made of
names and numbers and requests
leaves circle stains like the bottom of a coffee mug
with the others on the space station desk.

i reset, undock, begin the trek to earth again *(the
definition of insanity—*
i know, i know.
survival and contentment mode
were my two only options for this run)

so we survive, except.
we are content, except for when
we scream so loud it shakes the sun

and everything else is found
in the space between the lines
where the dragons' breaths mingle
even as they reach

and a really shitty xylophone
does the absolute best it can
under circumstance and stage lights for
a cosmic auditorium's captive audience

(we are still here
in the pitch-black moments
           before anyone applauds.)

TENDING CLAY; UNEARTHING STARS

memory (iii)

*i want to be kept
like a little red penguin
kept; the opposite
of every second i spend running
kept. in the way i've not yet learned
to keep myself*

side effect profile: oculogyric crisis

i don't want to write poems today
and yet, well, here i am
because i think today i'm scared
and this is all i know to do
like praying
like looking to the sky and saying
i believe in you
you wild thing that is not blue
i am not blue either; i'm
not sure that i am much of anything at all

i'm certainly not sight
not when my eyes are rolling up and hiding
just behind my brows
not light
my bones cemented at the joints;
tethered to the ground with floss
not *take my hand and run*
not *damn the consequences*
(a little too much *damn the consequences*)

not enough manic
not enough pixie
not enough dream and
not enough girl

TENDING CLAY; UNEARTHING STARS

other girls can damn their consequences;
mine are damning me instead
calling, calling, calling;
                    i let them go to voicemail

grief (iii)

i lost my voice in the drowning
the down
        down
                downing
i swallowed saltwater
even as it swallowed me
i kicked my feet
and cast my arms about
and learned to breathe the water
and thought i had been taught to swim

TENDING CLAY; UNEARTHING STARS

once, its name was phoenix

*i remember being well
but only like a story; the fire took the rest
all i know tonight is weak, and what it is
to wobble as i stand
this baby bird
this ghost of phoenix-past, and phoenix-yet-to-be,
is one who rises from the ashes
with a bit too much smoke
left in its lungs.*

*i remember water
rolling off the back of an old husk,
a shell built over many days of spring and rocks,
gentle grass and balmy river
(a place one could forget ones name was phoenix)
that husk has been torn off, and whether
too soon, like a scab, or just in time, like molting skin,
this new self underneath is tender in its infant stage
and leaves me shivering under thin and ashy feathers.*

*i live and i remember what it is to live (i think)
i rise, and think that i remember
that part too
?*

MJ ANTHONY

but one cannot go
from flames to flight
in an instant, so,
           please

as the sun sets on our anger, let the fire cool,
let us rest in the embers, swaddled up in warmth
under the ghost of wider wings
let rising be for morning
and let the ghosts
of flames-been and birds-to-be
           both rest
in the rage-free grief
of meanwhile.

interlude (ii)

today i would be angry
if the breathing did not hurt so much
angry at the home i have
its timbers made of flesh and bones
angry at the body's
origami joints and heavy stones
angry at the ocean, angry at the clouds
angry, angry, angry
(but i'm not, g.dd.mn i'm not
and you can tell with every word)
today i want to
want to be
alive enough for anger
not to fully empty me

memory (iv)

tonight i am not she or they or he
i am 'do not refer to me'
i am afraid
and fearing takes my fragile thread to humanness
and stretches it
and i can call the ocean she
but not a single wave—how can
i isolate an echo from the air that fills the cave?
thus how can i be anything tonight?
tonight when i am sick,
when i am barely clinging on to 'me'?
tonight i've drifted off into the sky
and when balloons have passed from sight
you no longer say 'look at them go'
you forget and get another, try again
and so, tomorrow, maybe i will
reevaluate.

(ask me again? again tomorrow, friend
i want to know the answers too.)

TENDING CLAY; UNEARTHING STARS

chryselephantine

could you hear me when i
howled at the moon and begged to
rend my body from this spine?
you were not listening, then.

surely though, you saw me when
each day i shed three skins; donned another four
linen tunics; woolen gowns
eleven times each equinox; twice that every Sunday.

perhaps at least you saw the workings of my
hands — those sketches full of masks and rips
and faces split in twain?
no? not even then?

then
i do not want to hear you speak to me.
not when i take the horns of those who'd gore me with
              them, crush them into ivory dust, and outline
every part of me deserving love in gold.

   you do not get a say the day i turn myself to art;
   you do not get a say when i discover what i've always
                                                  been.

does money buy happiness?
(on habitat requirements)

Money buys conditioner, dye, developer; bleach.

Money buys the soap and money pays the water bill. Money buys new clothes, the kind you feel yourself in. It buys the first deodorant you pick yourself, and the one after, too, and the one after three, until you smell like green apple or white tea, and decide that this is right, that this is you.

Money pays your first apartment's rent, over and over again each month. It buys fights with your roommates, pays for losing trust. It buys the hours of the truck you use to move.

Money buys your second apartment too, a complicated knot of a place with a dying garden in the back and thriving hedges in the front and a laundry machine in the basement you hardly ever use because it charges two dollars a load and the dryer doesn't work unless you run it twice (that's six.)

Money does buy the engagement ring, the time in Maine, the tidal pools, the little crabs you see.

TENDING CLAY; UNEARTHING STARS

Money does not buy the love you have, tonight-untainted feeling that wells up inside your chest as their head lies on the pillow next to you, clicking softly as they settle back to sleep.

Money does not buy them; does not buy you.
It doesn't buy the mornings before work, those ones where either chance or luck finds both of you awake. Does not buy the summers where the two of you can hardly stand to touch in the oppressive heat. Does not buy the winters where you cuddle closer, closer, closer to one body than to "you" and "me." Does not buy the kisses under blankets or your circled arms and happy stimming feet.

But money? *oh, the money, friend.*
The money buys the sheets.

appetite

*my stomach is a ravenous thing
who growls and snarls inside of me
and it should not have taken me 21 years
to call it disordered, when
i heard her cries and called them good.*

he(e/a)ling

lately i've been skipping meals—but
is it skipping to just
t e a s e them on? stringing
them along like treats you'd give a dog?

"stand a little taller"

"sit a little longer"

"lay a little flatter to the floor"

(*obey me, obey me,* **obey me**)

i am still learning how
to learn to treat my stomach
like a dog, all the way

that is, like a friend
who deserves to eat, no matter what,
and to be spoken to in gentle voice
cooed at and cuddled
and *loved*

seasonal dormancy

the summer sun beats down and renders all
in hazy stupor
and it reminds me
of too many hot days
wanting to separate from my skin
and peel apart from my spine.

the autumn trees loosen their grip on their leaves
shedding all the frills that do not fit them anymore
and it reminds me that
these branches, even stripped of leaves
are beautiful
and i wait a little less
before i loose my hold on mine.

the birds fly south to a gentler place
to grow in ways that winter here would not allow them
and it reminds me of too long
spent plowing frozen soil, convinced;
convincing that my pain was fine.

in spring,
the flowers bloom, and the buds rise
and it reminds me

TENDING CLAY; UNEARTHING STARS

of growing and of healing and discovering
that i could also bring some springtime
to my mind.

abluvion

after i turn the tap and stop the
beating of the water on my frame
little flecks of skin
unravel themselves from
                      my shoulders, biceps, hips, the
valley in the center of my chest.

in a moment, panic
overwhelms me and i scrub
n scrub n scrub n scrub
           (until everything i have been holding
                                 can be free
      of everything that has been holding onto me)

on life expectancy
(again)

i think i was young, as a girl, or that
i was mostly-a-girl when i was younger, and
i'm sort of sitting on that fence right now
happy in my overalls and heels

for better or worse
i was planted, sprouted, watered
as a girl would be
and whether or not it took, i
don't think i would change those things
you know?

none of us get do-overs, but
i go back and forth on wanting one
when all the kids i went to high school with
are going to each others' weddings
kids at home; dates in tow
looking like adults we used to know

and like, i sort-of thought that if

a.) i never went ahead, i couldn't
leave them all behind

or maybe if

b.) i grew up too, i wouldn't feel so badly like
a kid who failed their swimming test
because they couldn't breathe
and had to spend the rest of camp restricted to
the shallow end

and while
my panic is still here, still
finding ways to show me i can also drown
while landlocked to familiar city streets
made up of sidewalks and cement,
a mile and six-tenths from water.

i think i might have been
a little failed
in ways besides the
"not-girl"
one

nuances of dysphoria

*i can't remember the last time i sat
and looked upon my skin.*

in winter i can go for days
changing clothes in stages as i live
in the same 3 hoodies and 5 jeans.

my body is a stranger
gorgeous—the way a movie extra is, but
here one shot and gone the next;
uncredited no matter how i search.

i run my hands across the lines and curves
as they shift in and out
of the territory of me:
*fuzzy legs, yes;
hips? unrecognizable*

it's like a statue
carved in marble through a blindfold
and i'm the pair of hands
grasping blindly in discovery
through slits in a box
in science class

MJ ANTHONY

i was never one for guessing games
easily bored
easily frustrated
easily convinced to throw out half the evidence
if half of it convinces me i'm right

i am the hands—never the object inside

*(i just want to know me
i just want to see)*

reflection (ii)

i sit with girlhood and- i feel- i *feel* —
*She's cupped between my palms like water, but
no matter how i try, hands pressed
edge to edge until the skin goes white, i feel it—*
girlhood just keeps weeping out

symbiosis

the earth and i are molting
and though we mark these days
by putting layers on, rather than
taking them off,
hidden does not mean gone
(whether we wish it to or not)

i take my cues from her, my earth, and
this is how we stay alive.
even when it is not what we were taught
choosing not to rake the leaves because
we believe it will be better
when she sheds her coats again
yawning like a cat
to roll and stretch in crunching leaves.
she'll turn her face and
bare her arms before the sun, to
let it shine on her again
let her bloom and rise and blush
let it shine, and let her
shine with it. even if it stings a little
she dances from the curtain to the call
sloughing on and off the weight
and does not lose herself

TENDING CLAY; UNEARTHING STARS

i'm proud of her;
i'm proud of me for watching,
letting hope come past my walls.

she'll reemerge
and i, like her
will too.

grief (iv)

the night i lost you
i had a good cry,
learned about deer,
heard their barking echo through
an unfamiliar wood,
and hoped you found that kind of freedom from our
rage.

planting myself

i wish i could go back
and tell my younger self to smile with her teeth
it wasn't your fault
the tick chose you; the doctor chose the drugs
and even if it were, you have every right
to bare your yellowed fangs and tell the world to move.
you are a tree, not to be picked
or potted for a lover
you are a wild thing
and it is time they stop dressing you up
in the clothes of a doll.

symptom profile: anhedonia

i take my meds with tea that tastes
"tea that tastes," a roommate used to say
(we are all anhedoniacs here)

they taste like salt and doctors offices and
death and life and three meals a day for
every day, for every week, for
every year and ~~ever, and ever~~
~~and ever and~~ my doctor asks me why
i got blood drawn two years ago
why i'm giving her results in question marks
why i asked for tests at all
and i don't have the words to say *because*
i can imagine lots of things but
feeling this for every day for every week for
ever (twice on sundays) isn't one of them

because i am getting sicker and better and
sicker and better and sicker again and i
have done this dance for thirteen years this fall

because at thirteen my body started
breaking and that is too young to be
catching every piece of you that falls
*and **i am running out of hands***

TENDING CLAY; UNEARTHING STARS

interlude (iii)
"brick by heavy. fucking. brick."

i am waiting for the earth to shake
waiting for the ground to break
waiting for the walls to shatter, lying
like my mind in crystals all around
for me to poke and prod and reassemble
if i can get up off the floor to do it

i am waiting for the world to change
in ways that feel a little more significant
than footfall after plodding footfall.

something new

this summer i have gone outside
and tanned in the sun
and that is something new
new, like a lover
new, like trusting
new, like staying still, unflinching
as the bees bumble past me to the heather
to the coriander, to the thyme
to the garden on the porch that is still beautiful
even the half of it that's not for me
(i am learning how it feels
to be okay with that)

this summer
the heat knocks me down, but not out
my bed claims me
but not as often as i leave it
i curl my fists around opportunity
and the monster on my shoulders stills
and trusts my judgment

i whisper that i want, i want
for the first time in my life *i want*
and the beast at my center nods
and asks before it holds me tight.

TENDING CLAY; UNEARTHING STARS

this summer
i am a little bit well
(praise god, at last)
i am better and worse
i am trying, learning, reaching for *a l i v e*
(praise god, my god at last)

stars in the night

it is something i am still trying to name
to watch a ceiling filled with moving things
as colors fade and fuzz
and live a man's whole life in half an hour
something, but i struggle to put it to words
(a picture's worth a thousand but i've
always been too much of a perfectionist
to finish what i start)

maybe something like a dance?
but in act three
(the place where things
are supposed to be resolved)
the music takes a darker shift
and i am fixed in place
with shadows whispering out of every corner.

it is something
a little less starry and a little more night
to walk in on the middle of a story
the shape familiar but the beats unknown
the man goes mad–*the man is gone*
you cannot change a thing–this time
he can't recover from it

TENDING CLAY; UNEARTHING STARS

it is something
to watch the worst bits first.

you can fast forward or rewind
both will take you back to – where we entered
stage door right — with the smiling guide –
neither one will change the –
green on the walls.
crows come next,
and roots and rot and – *outcome* – and —

my lover looks at me,
a question in their eyes
it's time to leave?

> not yet, i think
> *not yet*, i say
> *i want to stay*

at least until the sunflowers come back again;

MJ ANTHONY

for my friends (hakanai)

how i wish that we had grown and met
                                in kinder worlds,
                                     ones upon
a gentler globe, a softer shore.   had learned to
keep our hearts unguarded without sacrifice.
a world that was, or is, or yet will be
not so set upon extinctions and extinct-ings
and more concerned with all the seconds
inbetween
                    (with every second and the way
          our endings make those inbetweens a gift)

TENDING CLAY; UNEARTHING STARS

the doctor says,
"keep doing what you're doing"

i count to 17
each morning when the days get bad
with teawater gone stale
with chocolate, with chips
with anything to lose the taste of words
like ashwaghanda; cardiotrophin,
cataplex and aripiprazole
words that mean not better
(words that mean not worse)

on life expectancy
(one more time)

my growing up was done as a girl
(it is what it was, we've
been through this before)
and,
to broach a newer thought,
i think my growing old
will be done as a man, but
in the middle of it all
there is just me
with not enough time
to try on everything
i want

abby laughed (or: i think adults should be allowed a toy (or sticker) for visiting the dentist (and/or chiropractor) too)

whenever i say shit / like *"i was a younger girl"*
/ or / *"the girl i was when i was young"* / i always
mean it / like we're also holding dialectic space
/ for when someone who's a girl / just sometimes
wants to be a boy / so hard / it hollows out their
throat / in aches / that no amount of ice-water
can sate /

/ and it's not that / being a boy would change
anything / you would still be / your mother's
daughter / and / your father's son / but something
indescribable / in the fabric of the universe /
/ might be fixed /

and god / you didn't even know / when you were
little / why you wanted to be a boy / or if
/ when it wouldn't change anything / or if
/ it would / change everything / i mean / you
didn't even know what it would mean / to be
a boy /

/ but then /

/ you never really understood / what it would

mean / to be a girl, either / except that everybody / seemed to think / that you were doing fine / at it / / so you wrote stories / playing princesses / and / glutted yourself on tales / of maidens in disguise /

/ and when your boobs grew in / and your blood slid out / you learned that one of the easiest ways / by far / to be a girl / was by being in pain /

/ and darling / you had always been / a little *too* good / at being in pain /

/ you told the receptionist / who let you color at her desk / while your mother had her bones / all wrestled back in place / that you were a woman now / all serious and important /

/ and when she laughed / and apologized / and laughed / nothing was clearer at all /

TENDING CLAY; UNEARTHING STARS

reflection (iii)

i am always looking through
a mirror dimly,
at girlhood; at myself
it is not a stretch
to grasp divinity (intangible)
from that

a retelling

i used to wonder why i was so in love
with the image and idea that sleeping beauty
never cared for musty towers, nor
long-hoarded secrets of the dead

no witch, no evil one conspired to take her agency;
she fled her room one summer day, and
pricked her finger on raspberry thorns.
the first pain she had ever been allowed to feel
was remembered only as an oddity, tempered by
the unmatched bliss of
fruit, picked straight from the sun-warmed earth,
just another curiosity of this thing called life.

in my story, she eats until full
and falls back laughing in the grass
until the afternoon sun lulls her to sleep
and the curse is not an ending, just a
transition
out of a home that was not hers
and into a world that is.

TENDING CLAY; UNEARTHING STARS

mountains

i took the beautiful mountains i was given
framed and under glass
and said *i want the real thing, thanks*
dug my hands into the earth and shaped
two peaks
sharp enough to cut, and
mounted them upon my collarbone
next, i went for something softer, like
that man would mow in circles for a dandelion
i've always wanted   something   like that
said about me too.
i spend my time in study,
practicing, perfecting
carving loops and whorls like fingerprints
across the time that i've been given
easy now, we stick the landing
palms slick on the controls.
because while i can name myself anew; make
pottery from clay– we won't survive
without the firing
*whereas i fear that i may break while being
thrown from kiln to kiln too many times*
i have to try these things for size
before i'll know if i can call them
home.

reflection (iv)

*happy, the day i dyed my hair myself
lives on in a purple ghost
on a bathroom wall
a day i looked in the mirror
and saw a glimpse of someone i could recognize*

TENDING CLAY; UNEARTHING STARS

stars (ii)
epilogue

the creatures whimper from their pins
and even as their blood dries on my hands
i hear them say,

to learn about ourself
was not intended as a punishment

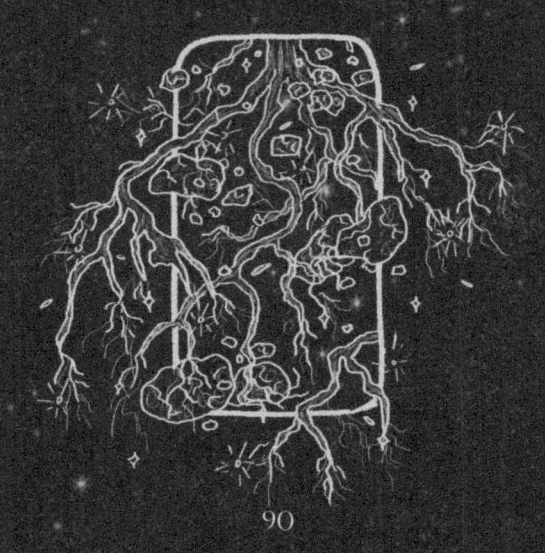

MJ ANTHONY

author's note:
on tending clay and unearthing stars

i really didn't think that of all the books i've put together over the last seven years, this one would be the hardest to stop writing.

a few days ago, my mother told me over the phone that she is surprised to still be learning about herself. in true, blunt, autistic form, i said that she should stop expecting to be done. as long as i remember, i've accepted that i will die still figuring pieces of myself out.

which leads me to now, agonizing over this author's letter because i am painfully aware that i am trying to pour the infinite wholeness of a self i'll never fully know into the finite vessel of a book that can only contain poems i've already written.

the poems speak for themselves, i think? so let me talk about the title:

all my life, my mother has had a garden. it wrapped around the house i grew up in, which was the house she grew up in, an old drafty thing on the south shore of Massachusetts. before it came into my grandparents hands, it used to be located just down the street, and for reasons lost to time, was carted down the street by horses to the place where it stands now.

the soil all around the house has been heavy with clay for as long as she's gardened in it, but things still grow. my childhood was full of chewing wild apple mint and weeding walking onions and avoiding poison ivy (and sumac, and oak). in the summers, there were black raspberries and white strawberries. when i got really into spices after college i learned that we had lavender and a yet-unidentified strain of oregano that i quickly became obsessed with.

TENDING CLAY; UNEARTHING STARS

that place has a lot of hurts tied to it. but it also has moments of joy and fleeting snatches of safety/stability that i am still trying to learn how to eke from an adult world set on killing anyone who cannot serve it. when healing means examining (cutting, forgiving, repotting) your roots, my body often feels like that house.

side note: after i moved out, the siding on the house i grew up in had to be replaced, and, due to carelessness in the process, all the soil surrounding the house was contaminated with lead from old paint. The soil, plants and all, has to be dug up and replaced, and nothing that grows there for the next X decades will be safe to consume. i am grieving this as best i know how. thank you, Effie, for immortalizing a few of my memories in the cover of this book. <3

so as we've covered, the story in this book can't be done until i am, but an open wound also can't heal until it closes. i think i'm done bleeding over this, and i hope these poems can be balm for you the way they have been stitches for me.

it's time to let the paint dry. let the bird rest, let the earth molt, let the tornado tear the walls to bits and let the bleeding creatures on the cork be freed and set down gently into garden soil. let the microcosm of these poems whirl and scream and settle somewhere safe i can revisit them; let them be contained within these covers so that i may be let go.

let the shit decompose, and let something else grow out of it.

not new, not perfect. just us.

and all the pages said, amen

Micah J Anthony

(January 2024)

hello friend!
as a thank you for reading this book & purchasing the paperback edition, you can download the ebook version in our store for free!

dragonbonepublishing.gumroad.com

un-myjq3s

acknowledgments

"brick by heavy fucking brick" which appears on p. 76 is a quote from the song GOOD MORNING SUNSHINE by The Narcissist Cookbook.

most of the pieces in this collection have been recycled from two previous books published under my childhood name. it would be impossible to list them all, since many have been split, spliced, edited, rewritten, and renamed, but if you read TREE (2021) or love & bees (2022), thanks for believing in me all this time. have fun with your literary analysis, and i hope you like the updates.

to Ziel, the love of my life, and my lawfully wedded wife as soon as the paperwork goes through. you have given me back so many pieces of myself, and there's no one i'd rather discover the rest of them with.

to Alroy, my chronic illness buddy: you're perfect and brilliant and i wish you were as enthusiastic about actually eating food as you are about mealtime punctuality, but in all other areas G-d broke the mold with you and i have no notes.

to Pippi, who i truly believe would kill for me if the occasion arose: please stop sitting on my lap fifteen minutes before i leave for work. i know you know i'm having a panic attack, unfortunately i do still have to put on pants.

to Bartholomeow, the cuddliest, sweetest, smartest asshole i've ever had the displeasure of carrying back down from the third floor landing. i hope you never change, and i hope we all survive it.

(for anyone concerned, the cats will be getting extra treats and smooches on their little heads tonight to compensate for the fact that they are illiterate)

to Nathaniel, who has been one of the biggest champions of me and my books, both on main and behind the scenes, since 2020– it's been incredible to watch your confidence, creativity, skill, and success all grow, and i'm so grateful to call you my friend.

to Effie, who said yes to Dragon Heart Press and put up with my bullshit in order to give me the most beautiful, perfect, fucking showstopping cover a debut collection could dream of– thank you for helping immortalize this piece of my life. i'm looking forward to seeing you in the next chapters!

to Sage– i am also pressing my forehead to yours like a cat!! thank you for trusting me with this Very Explicitly Labeled Harpoon

to Sidney– thank you for your safety, your shelter, your support, and your science/foraging knowledge. you're one of the coolest people i am lucky enough to know!!

to all my early readers (Beca, Rae, Gracie, Dawn, Joy, Sage, Annaka, Myles, Matt, and Tom), as well as everyone in the gay lil poets discord server– my love and appreciation for you all is boundless. y'all carried (& are still carrying) me through this process with your enthusiasm and kind words, and i couldn't have asked for a better community around me.

to everyone whose gentleness, patience, forgiveness, and love has gotten me this far. i am so blessed by you <3

If you enjoyed this collection, you might like these other titles!

Unleash the Cosmos: A Space Poetry Anthology
edited by Nathaniel Luscombe and Jenni Sauer

Discover a spaceship in your backyard, send your run-on wishes into space, take a bite of space toast, and drink some starlight on tap.

These fifty poems are a love letter to the vast variety of emotions we experience when thinking about the universe. You're invited to find a cozy spot, look up at the stars, take a deep breath, and revel in the wonders, hope, fear, and heartbreak of the endless cosmos.

Perfect for fans of Nathaniel Luscombe, Becky Chambers, and Alex Silvius.

When One World Ends, Another Begins
by Nathaniel Luscombe

"Words became my bloodletting. I've been bleeding now for years."

At times playful, at times heartbreaking, *When One World Ends, Another Begins* is a raw, honest look at how it feels to be alive. On the surface, these poems are an examination of what it is to be human. Underneath, they're an exploration of body image, fear, faith, and the ways life runs in circles. They exist to peel back the tough layers and expose the softness inside.

About the Author

MJ Anthony (they/them) is a queer, trans, and disabled poet + storyteller. Some days they are incapacitated by several of their disabling conditions, including premenstrual dysphoric disorder (PMDD), OCD, and post treatment lyme disease. Other days they get to be a caretaker at a local community library, and co-run Dragon Heart Press with their friend Nathaniel. All those days find them living in Boston with their wife, three cats, and a very lovely leopard gecko named Tumbleweed.
Micah has a passion for independent publishing, speculative fiction, high pulp orange juice, and unsweetened black tea.

You can find them on instagram **@sparrowsurviving**, or check out their current happenings at **mjanthony.carrd.co**